KEW POCKETBOOKS

CACTI

Introduction by Olwen M. Grace
Curated by Lydia White

Kew Publishing
Royal Botanic Gardens, Kew

KEW HOLDS ONE OF THE LARGEST COLLECTIONS of botanical literature, art and archive material in the world. The library comprises 185,000 monographs and rare books, around 150,000 pamphlets, 5,000 serial titles and 25,000 maps. The Archives contain vast collections relating to Kew's long history as a global centre of plant information and a nationally important botanic garden including 7 million letters, lists, field notebooks, diaries and manuscript pages.

The Illustrations Collection comprises 200,000 watercolours, oils, prints and drawings, assembled over the last 200 years, forming an exceptional visual record of plants and fungi. Works include those of the great masters of botanical illustration such as Ehret, Redouté and the Bauer brothers, Thomas Duncanson, George Bond and Walter Hood Fitch. Our special collections include historic and contemporary originals prepared for *Curtis's Botanical Magazine*, the work of Margaret Meen, Thomas Baines, Margaret Mee, Joseph Hooker's Indian sketches, Edouard Morren's bromeliad paintings, 'Company School' works commissioned from Indian artists by Roxburgh, Wallich, Royle and others, and the Marianne North Collection, housed in the gallery named after her in Kew Gardens.

INTRODUCTION

CACTI ARE AMONG THE MOST INSTANTLY
recognisable plant forms. Swollen with water and
embellished with sharp spines or hairs, and ranging
from tall columnar towering forms to rotund barrel cacti
and prickly pears with flattened paddle-like stems, cacti
have become icons of desert habitats. Their large, open,
and often scented flowers are a crowning glory.

Cacti belong to the Cactaceae, one of the largest
flowering plant families, which contains over 1,800
species. The vast majority are cacti in the strict sense,
classified by taxonomists in the subfamily Cacteae. They
are found primarily on the American subcontinents,
from the southern tip of Argentina to Canada, and in
the Caribbean. One genus, *Rhipsalis*, travelled to Africa,
Madagascar and Sri Lanka. Cacti are not restricted to
deserts: specialised tissues inside the plant provide a
reservoir of water that allows them to thrive in many
harsh habitats where plants contend with extreme
temperature, sun and water fluctuations, from coastal
plains to high mountain tops.

The origins of the distinctive cactus life form have puzzled botanists. Cacti are absent from the fossil record: soft, water-storing tissues are not well preserved as fossils. However, clues from the family tree of living cacti suggest that the earliest cacti were leafy trees and shrubs growing in tropical or perhaps semiarid habitats. Their transformation to the extraordinary architectural forms showcased on the pages of this book is thought to have happened after the characteristic water reservoir tissues evolved in ancestral cacti.

Plant species with finely tuned adaptations to very particular habitats are sensitive to climate change and disturbance. The risk of extinction is, therefore, grave for many cacti species and they are widely protected by local and international laws to ensure that wild populations can persist unchallenged by humans. The best source for acquiring cacti to grow at home is a reputable nursery.

Cacti are brought into people's lives by their firm popularity as decorative houseplants and ornamental garden plants for landscaping in dry places. A cactus nurtured on a windowsill is often the beginning of a lifelong passion for plants. Cacti are easy to grow and the most avid collectors are drawn to their extraordinary diversity of species.

At Kew, cacti are displayed in the Princess of Wales Conservatory's arid zones. They are well represented in both the living collections and preserved reference collections in the Herbarium, supporting research and conservation by scientists at Kew and partner organisations.

Olwen M. Grace
Senior Research Leader,
Comparative Plant & Fungal Biology,
Royal Botanic Gardens, Kew

Ferocactus viridescens

coast barrel cactus,
San Diego barrel cactus

---

from Karl Schumann,
Max Gürke, and F. Vaupel *Blühende Kakteen
(Iconographia Cactacearum)*, 1904–1921

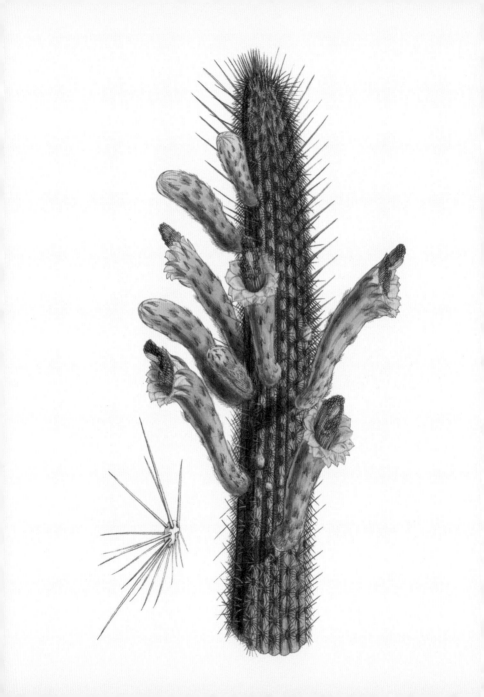

Cleistocactus baumannii

firecracker cactus

by Walter Hood Fitch
from *Curtis's Botanical Magazine,* 1850

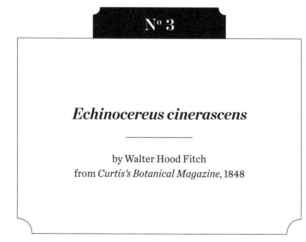

N° 3

Echinocereus cinerascens

by Walter Hood Fitch
from *Curtis's Botanical Magazine,* 1848

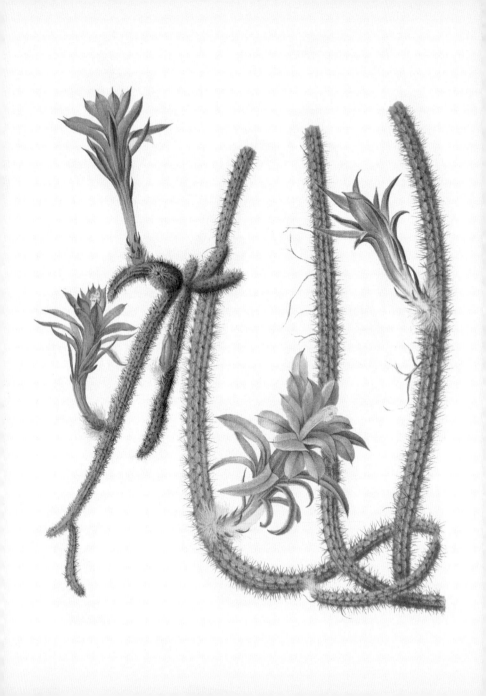

Aporocactus flagelliformis

rat's tail cactus

by M. E. Eaton and A. A. Newton
from Nathaniel Lord Britton and Joseph
Nelson Rose *The Cactaceae: descriptions and
illustrations of plants of the cactus family*, 1919–23

Selenicereus grandiflorus

night-blooming cereus,
queen of the night

---

by Joseph Constantine Stadler
from Robert John Thornton *Temple of Flora*,
1799–1810

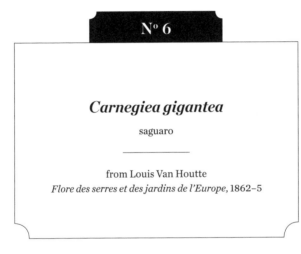

Carnegiea gigantea

saguaro

from Louis Van Houtte
Flore des serres et des jardins de l'Europe, 1862–5

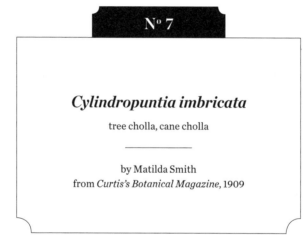

Nº 7

Cylindropuntia imbricata

tree cholla, cane cholla

———————

by Matilda Smith
from *Curtis's Botanical Magazine*, 1909

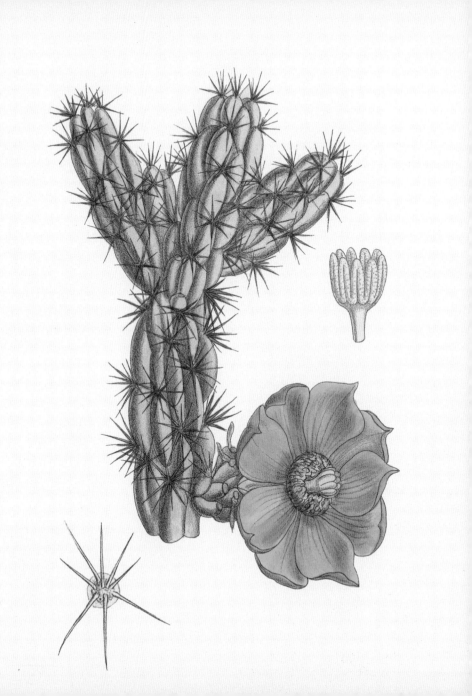

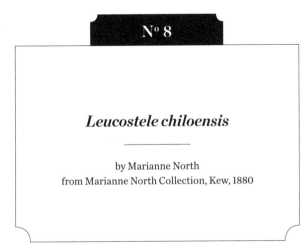

Leucostele chiloensis

by Marianne North
from Marianne North Collection, Kew, 1880

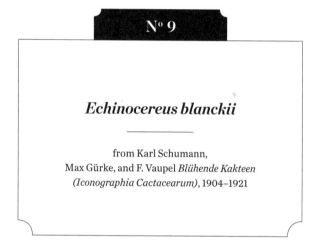

Echinocereus blanckii

from Karl Schumann,
Max Gürke, and F. Vaupel *Blühende Kakteen
(Iconographia Cactacearum)*, 1904–1921

Echinopsis aurea (1),
Copiapoa coquimbana (2),
Lophophora williamsii (3 & 4)

golden Easter lily cactus, golden cob (1),
peyote, dumpling cactus (3 & 4)

by M. E. Eaton
from Nathaniel Lord Britton and Joseph
Nelson Rose *The Cactaceae: descriptions and
illustrations of plants of the cactus family*, 1919–23

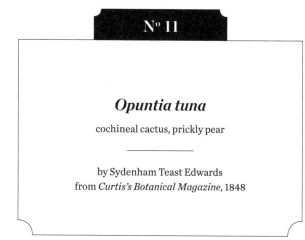

N° 11

Opuntia tuna

cochineal cactus, prickly pear

by Sydenham Teast Edwards
from *Curtis's Botanical Magazine,* 1848

Copiapoa marginata

by Walter Hood Fitch
from *Curtis's Botanical Magazine*, 1851

Schlumbergera truncata

Christmas cactus,
Thanksgiving cactus, holiday cactus

from Édouard Morren *La Belgique Horticole*, 1866

Nº 14

Pelecyphora aselliformis

hatchet cactus

by Walter Hood Fitch

from *Curtis's Botanical Magazine*, 1873

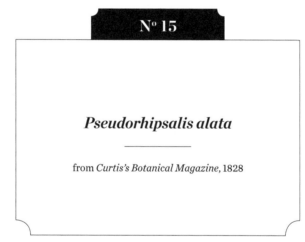

N⁰ 15

Pseudorhipsalis alata

from *Curtis's Botanical Magazine,* 1828

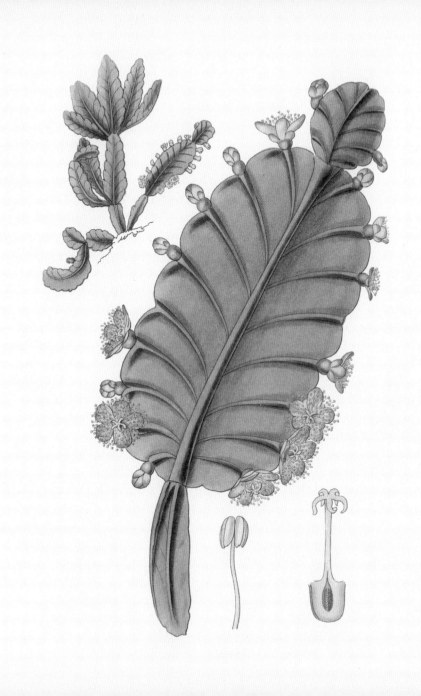

Echinocactus platyacanthus

giant barrel cactus

---

from Louis Van Houtte
Flore des serres et des jardins de l'Europe, 1850

Nº 17

Echinocactus rhodophthalmus

by Walter Hood Fitch
from *Curtis's Botanical Magazine*, 1850

N° 18

Consolea moniliformis

from Michel Étienne Descourtilz
Flore médicale des Antilles, 1821

Cereus hildmannianus

hedge cactus

———————

from Nathaniel Lord Britton and
Joseph Nelson Rose *The Cactaceae: descriptions
and illustrations of plants of the cactus family*, 1919–23

Astrophytum myriostigma

bishop's cap

from Karl Schumann,
Max Gürke, and F. Vaupel *Blühende Kakteen
(Iconographia Cactacearum)*, 1904–1921

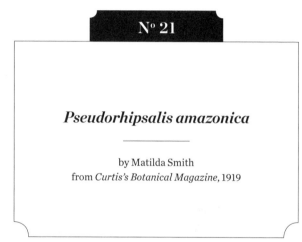

Pseudorhipsalis amazonica

by Matilda Smith

from *Curtis's Botanical Magazine*, 1919

Carnegiea gigantea

saguaro

from Joseph Trimble Rothrock
*Reports upon the botanical collections made
in portions of Nevada, Utah, California, Colorado,
New Mexico and Arizona,* 1878

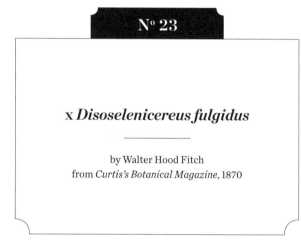

N° 23

x *Disoselenicereus fulgidus*

by Walter Hood Fitch
from *Curtis's Botanical Magazine*, 1870

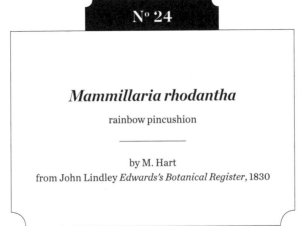

Mammillaria rhodantha

rainbow pincushion

---

by M. Hart

from John Lindley *Edwards's Botanical Register*, 1830

Harrisia divaricata

from Michel Étienne Descourtilz
Flore médicale des Antilles, 1821

Pilosocereus leucocephalus

old man cactus

from Karl Schumann,
Max Gürke, and F. Vaupel *Blühende Kakteen
(Iconographia Cactacearum)*, 1904–1921

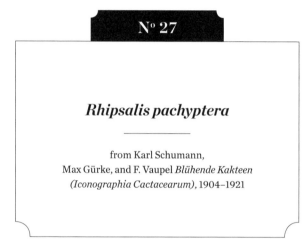

Rhipsalis pachyptera

from Karl Schumann,
Max Gürke, and F. Vaupel *Blühende Kakteen
(Iconographia Cactacearum)*, 1904–1921

Echinocereus engelmannii (1),
Echinopsis maximiliana (2),
Echinopsis pentlandii (3),
Echinopsis lateritia (4)

torch cactus, strawberry cactus (1)

———————

by M. E. Eaton
from Nathaniel Lord Britton and Joseph
Nelson Rose *The Cactaceae: descriptions and
illustrations of plants of the cactus family*, 1919–23

Echinocereus dasyacanthus

Texas rainbow cactus

---

from Karl Schumann,
Max Gürke, and F. Vaupel *Blühende Kakteen
(Iconographia Cactacearum)*, 1904–1921

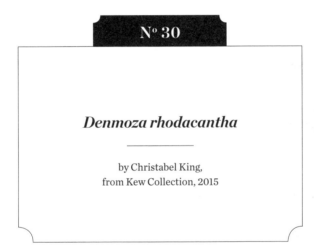

N⁰ 30

Denmoza rhodacantha

by Christabel King,
from Kew Collection, 2015

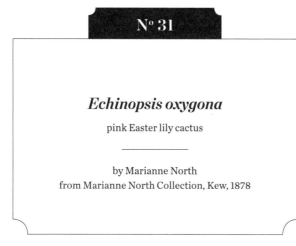

Echinopsis oxygona

pink Easter lily cactus

---

by Marianne North
from Marianne North Collection, Kew, 1878

Nº 32

Mammillaria mammillaris

woolly nipple cactus

---

from Johannes Commelin
*Horti medici Amstelodamensis rariorum
tam Orientalis,* 1697–1701

Pilosocereus royenii

pipe organ cactus

———————

by W. J. Hooker

from *Curtis's Botanical Magazine*, 1832

Echinocereus berlandieri

Berlandier's hedgehog cactus

from Karl Schumann,
Max Gürke, and F. Vaupel *Blühende Kakteen
(Iconographia Cactacearum)*, 1904–1921

N° 35

Ferocactus hamatacanthus

Mexican fruit cactus,
Texas barrel cactus

———————

by Walter Hood Fitch
from *Curtis's Botanical Magazine*, 1852

Neolloydia conoidea

cone cactus, Chihuahuan beehive

———————

from Karl Schumann,
Max Gürke, and F. Vaupel *Blühende Kakteen
(Iconographia Cactacearum)*, 1904–1921

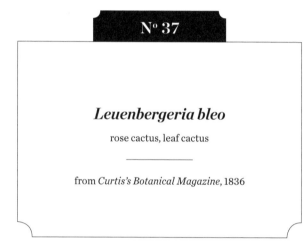

Leuenbergeria bleo

rose cactus, leaf cactus

———————

from *Curtis's Botanical Magazine,* 1836

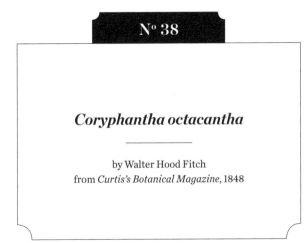

N° 38

Coryphantha octacantha

by Walter Hood Fitch
from *Curtis's Botanical Magazine*, 1848

Ariocarpus retusus

cobbler's thumb

---

from Karl Schumann,
Max Gürke, and F. Vaupel *Blühende Kakteen
(Iconographia Cactacearum)*, 1904–1921

Echinocereus scheeri

by Matilda Smith
from *Curtis's Botanical Magazine*, 1906

ILLUSTRATION SOURCES

Books and Journals

Bartlett, John Russell (1854). *Personal narrative of explorations and incidents in Texas, New Mexico, California, Sonora, and Chihuahua.* G. Routledge, London; D. Appleton, New York.

Britton, Nathaniel Lord and Rose, Joseph Nelson (1919–23). *The Cactaceae: descriptions and illustrations of plants of the cactus family.* The Carnegie Institution of Washington, Washington.

Commelin, Johannes (1697–1701). *Horti medici Amstelodamensis rariorum tam Orientalis.* P. Apud and J. Blaeu, Amsterdam.

Descourtilz, Michel Étienne (1821). *Flore médicale des Antilles.* Chez Corsnier, Paris.

Hooker, J. D. (1870). *Cereus fulgidus. Curtis's Botanical Magazine.* Volume 96, t. 5856.

Hooker, J. D. (1873). *Pelecyphora aselliformis* var. *concolor. Curtis's Botanical Magazine.* Volume 99, t. 6061.

Hooker, W. J. (1828). *Cactus alatus. Curtis's Botanical Magazine.* Volume 55, t. 2820.

Hooker, W. J. (1832). *Cereus royeni. Curtis's Botanical Magazine.* Volume 59, t. 3125.

Hooker, W. J. (1836). *Pereskia bleo. Curtis's Botanical Magazine.* Volume 63, t. 3478.

Hooker, W. J. (1848). *Echinocactus chlorophthalmus. Curtis's Botanical Magazine.* Volume 74, t. 4373.

Hooker, W. J. (1848). *Mamillaria clava. Curtis's Botanical Magazine.* Volume 74, t. 4358.

Hooker, W. J. (1850). *Cereus tweediei. Curtis's Botanical Magazine.* Volume 76, t. 4498.

Hooker, W. J. (1850). *Echinocactus rhodophthalmus. Curtis's Botanical Magazine.* Volume 76, t. 4486.

Hooker, W. J. (1851). *Echinocactus streptocaulon. Curtis's Botanical Magazine.* Volume 77, t. 4562.

Hooker, W. J. (1852). *Echinocactus longihamathus. Curtis's Botanical Magazine.* Volume 78, t. 4632.

Lindley, John (1830). *Mamillaria pulchra. Edwards's Botanical Register.* Volume 16, t. 1329.

Lindley, J. (1833). *The Crimson Creeping Cereus. Edwards's Botanical Register.* Volume 19, t. 1565.

Morren, Édouard (1866). *Epiphyllum truncatum. La Belgique Horticole.* Volume 16, p. 257.

Prain, D. (1909). *Opuntia imbricata. Curtis's Botanical Magazine.* Volume 135, t. 8290.

Prain, D. (1919). *Wittia panamensis. Curtis's Botanical Magazine.* Volume 145, t. 8799.

Rothrock, J. T. (1878). *Reports upon the botanical collections made in portions of Nevada, Utah, California, Colorado, New Mexico and Arizona.* The United States Government Publishing Office, Washington.

Schumann, Karl, Gürke, Max and Vaupel, F. (1904–1921). *Blühende Kakteen (Iconographia Cactacearum).* Neudamm, J. Neumann, Melsungen.

Sims, J. (1813). *Cactus tuna. Curtis's Botanical Magazine.* Volume 37-8, t. 1557.

Thiselton-Dyer, W. T. (1906). *Cereus scheerii. Curtis's Botanical Magazine.* Volume 132, t. 8096.

Thornton, Robert John (1799–1810). *Temple of Flora, or Garden of Nature.* T. Bensley, London.

Van Houtte, Louis (1850). *Echinocactus visnaga. Flore des serres et des jardins de l'Europe.* Volume 6, p. 265.

Van Houtte, Louis (1862–5). *Cereus giganteus. Flore des serres et des jardins de l'Europe.* Volume 15, p. 187.

Art Collections

Marianne North (1830–90) – comprising over 800 oils on paper, showing plants in their natural settings, painted by North, who recorded the world's flora during travels from 1871 to 1885, with visits to 16 countries in 5 continents. The main collection is on display in the Marianne North Gallery at Kew Gardens, bequeathed by North and built according to her instructions, first opened in 1882.

FURTHER READING

Anderson, Miles (2002). *World Encyclopedia of Cacti and Succulents.* Hermes House, London.

Britton, Nathaniel Lord and Rose, Joseph Nelson (1919–23). *The Cactaceae: descriptions and illustrations of plants of the cactus family.* The Carnegie Institution of Washington, Washington.

Charles, Graham (2003). *Cacti and succulents: an illustrated guide to the plants and their cultivation.* The Crowood Press, Ramsbury.

North, Marianne and Mills, Christopher. (2018). *Marianne North: The Kew Collection.* Royal Botanic Gardens, Kew.

Payne, Michelle. (2016). *Marianne North: A Very Intrepid Painter.* Revised edition. Royal Botanic Gardens, Kew.

Thornton, Robert John (2008). *The Temple of Flora.* Facsimile edition of the original. Taschen, Köln.

Willis, Kathy and Fry, Carolyn. (2014). *Plants from Roots to Riches.* John Murray, London in association with the Royal Botanic Gardens, Kew.

Online

www.biodiversitylibrary.org The world's largest open access digital library specialising in biodiversity and natural history literature and archives, including many rare books.

www.kew.org Royal Botanic Gardens, Kew website with information on Kew's science, collections and visitor programme.

www.plantsoftheworldonline.org An online database providing authoritative information of the world's flora gathered from the botanical literature published over the last 250 years.

ACKNOWLEDGEMENTS

Kew Publishing would like to thank the following for their help with this publication: Kew succulent expert Olwen Grace; in the Library, Art and Archives, Fiona Ainsworth; for digitisation work, Paul Little; for permission to use her illustration on page 68, botanical artist, Christabel King.

INDEX

First published in 2020
Royal Botanic Gardens, Kew,
Richmond, Surrey, TW9 3AB, UK
www.kew.org

ISBN 978 1 84246 712 1

Distributed on behalf of the Royal Botanic Gardens, Kew in North America by the University of Chicago Press, 1427 East 60th St, Chicago, IL 60637, USA.

British Library Cataloguing in Publication Data
A catalogue record for this book is available from the British Library

Design and page layout: Ocky Murray
Image work: Christine Beard
Production Manager: Jo Pillai
Copy-editing: Michelle Payne

Printed and bound in Italy by Printer Trento srl.

MIX
Paper from
responsible sources
FSC® C015829

Front cover image: *Ferocactus hamatacanthus* (see page 78)

Endpapers: *Carnegiea gigantea*, saguaro from John Russell Bartlett *Personal narrative of explorations and incidents in Texas, New Mexico, California, Sonora, and Chihuahua*, 1854

p2: *Cereus* sp., saguaro from John Russell Bartlett *Personal narrative of explorations and incidents in Texas, New Mexico, California, Sonora, and Chihuahua*, 1854

p4: *Thelocactus bicolor*, glory of Texas from Karl Schumann, Max Gürke, and F. Vaupel *Blühende Kakteen (Iconographia Cactacearum)*, 1904–1921

p8: *Carnegiea gigantea*, saguaro by Marianne North, from Marianne North Collection, Kew, 1875

p93: *Disocactus speciosus*, sun cereus, nopalillo by Sarah Anne Drake, from John Lindley Edwards's *Botanical Register*, 1833

For information or to purchase all Kew titles please visit shop.kew.org/kewbooksonline or email publishing@kew.org

Kew's mission is to be the global resource in plant and fungal knowledge and the world's leading botanic garden.

Kew receives approximately one third of its funding from Government through the Department for Environment, Food and Rural Affairs (Defra). All other funding needed to support Kew's vital work comes from members, foundations, donors and commercial activities, including book sales.

Publishers note about names
The scientific names of the plants featured in this book are current, Kew accepted names at the time of going to press. They may differ from those used in original-source publications. The common names given are those most often used in the English language, or sometimes vernacular names used for the plants in their native countries.